Computer-Assisted Language Learning for Deaf Children

a natural language interface system

Robert Ward

Originally titled "Computer-Assisted Learning for the Deaf", a dissertation submitted to the Faculty of Technology, University of Manchester, as partial fulfilment of the requirements for the Degree of Master of Science, by R.D.Ward, B.A. Psychology (University of Hull).

Department of Computation, University of Manchester Institute of Science and Technology, 1981.

Published in this form January 2010 by Robert David Ward, Shepley, Huddersfield, U.K.

ISBN 978-1-4452-7492-8

FORWARD TO THIS EDITION

This scanned copy of the original dissertation, specifies a set of computer programs to allow learners to interact with a computer through written language. It sets out the foundations of an approach later investigated in a Ph.D. thesis, "Natural Language, Computer-Assisted Learning and Language-Impaired Children", by the same author, at the Department of Psychology, University of Hull, U.K., in 1987.

Robert Ward, Shepley, Huddersfield. January 2010.

DECLARATION

No portion of the work referred to in this dissertation has been submitted in support of an application for another degree or qualification of this or any other university or other institution of learning.

ACKNOWLEDGEMENTS

I would like to thank my supervisors, **Dr. Paul Arnold** of the Department of Psychology, University of Manchester and **Dr. Stephen Young** of the Department of Computation, University of Manchester Institute of Science and Technology for their interest and support during the preparation of this dissertation.

2

ABSTRACT

Initial work on a "language-understanding",
computer-assisted-learning system for helping to teach
reading and writing to deaf children ("LUCALD") is
reported and discussed. The system interacts with the
learner through simple written language and provides
feedback about the lexical, syntactic and semantic
acceptability of sentences constructed by the learner.
The rationale for this approach, based upon psycholinguistic theory, is outlined.

Interaction occurs within a domain of meaning
defined by external pictures. These are computationally
represented in a "dictionary" file which contains
lexical, syntactic and semantic information. Syntax is
represented by a finite-state-grammar network diagram.
Alternative domains and syntax diagrams may be substituted.

The system consists of an analysis and feedback
program plus service programs. The service programs
are used to construct alternative external dictionaries
and syntax files for use by the main program. The
tutorial aspects of the system remain undeveloped.

COMPUTER ASSISTED LEARNING FOR THE DEAF

'LUCALD' : A "language-understanding", computer assisted learning system for helping to teach reading and writing to deaf children.

Chapter I : The reading and writing abilities of deaf children.

Although it is well known that deaf children find speech
difficult to learn, it is not generally realised that
their difficulties apply to a whole range of language
skills.   These include reading and writing. Because
the degree of difficulty relates to the degree of hearing
loss and to the age of onset of deafness, most difficulty is
experienced by the profoundly ,prelingually deaf. This dissertation applies mainly to this group of people.

It is difficult not to understate the severity of the reading
and writing problems of the profoundly ,prelingually deaf.
Conrad(1977) found that 35% of these people fail to achieve
a reading age of 7 and therefore fall within the Department
of Education and Science's definition of illiteracy. A further
20% fail to achieve the average reading ability of normal 9-
year olds and are therefore within the DES definition of semi-
literacy.   In all, 75% never reach a reading age of 13.   In
effect , this means that most profoundly, prelingually deaf
people are unable to understand newspapers, books or the tele-
vision subtitles specifically intended for the deaf.   It has
been estimated , for example, that out of approximately 200
deaf adults in the City of Hull, only 3 have sufficient reading
ability to understand a novel (Francksen 1980).

Detailed examination of the written language of deaf children
shows that the low reading ages reflect a failure to master
many basic aspects of vocabulary, morphology, syntax and semantics.   Purely accretional measures such as size of vocabulary give some idea of the magnitude of the problem. Dale(1974)
reports that the mean vocabulary of normal 5-year-olds is 2000

words. The average of all 5 year olds in special schools for the deaf is 250 and in the profoundly, prelingually deaf may be only 25. But such figures do not demonstrate the entirety of the problem. Even if a particular word is within the vocabulary of a deaf child, his knowledge of language may be insufficient to use the word other than in a disconnected way.

The child may be unable to convert the word into related morphological forms. Bunch and Clarke (1978) found that few profoundly deaf children below the age of 12 have mastered the rules for making plural nouns from singular ones. Even with older children aged 13 to 17, only one in three could form '-s' plurals and one in six '-es' plurals. Similar inabilities were found with respect to the construction of past participles '-ed', the present progressive '-ing' and the third person singular '- s '. Although Arnold (1981) suggests that this may be an overly dismal picture resulting from certain aspects of Bunch and Clarke's methodology, it nevertheless seems clear that profoundly deaf children do experience severe difficulties with simple morphological rules.

Another feature of the language of profoundly deaf children is poor syntactic ability. Myklebust's 'picture Story Language Test' (1965) demonstrates very well the kinds of errors which occur in spontaneous writing. In order of frequency the four most common types of error are omissions, substitutions, additions and word order. The following examples are typical:-

1. The boy playing   'is' omitted.
2. A boy will playing   'will' substituted for 'is'.
3. A boy is be playing   'be' added.
4. A boy playing is   'is' and 'playing' transposed.

Myklebust's test is not without problems. Often syntax is so deviant that it is impossible to count the errors (VandenBerg 1971), but again it seems clear that errors of a fundamental nature are involved. The following sample of the spontaneous writing of a 15 year old boy with a hearing loss of 94 dB shows just how deviant, or possibly non-existent, the syntax can be. The sample was obtained by Arnold (1978) using one of Myklebust's pictures which shows a boy playing with dolls and toy furniture;

"book chair doll table coat boak boy dog shirt car
box house door I have boy and doll pong horse boy
two girl one eye ear have want work wood goll chair
small chair two small chair two big box big wood big
door table big dog small big boy wall big wood big
door table big dog small big boy wall big in the
jup cup knift four pour and big door hose car small
window eggs girl chair ball coats shoot tie dog
eggslone car boat one"

The words are appropriate and most are correctly spelt, but syntax is minimal. Arnold (1981, 1978) discusses other studies of the syntactic abilities of deaf children. These include those of Bunch (1979) and Quigley et al (1977). Bunch found that deaf children have difficulty in correcting sentences which contain syntax errors. Quigley's 'Test of Syntactic Abilities' showed widespread misuse and misunderstanding of a whole range of elementary grammatical concepts including the definite article, verb forms, subject-verb agreement, interstitial words, passive sentences, negative sentences and question formation. Quigley et al conclude that such poor control of syntax makes full semantic understanding unlikely.

This brief chapter is not intended to provide a comprehensive review of the reading and writing abilities of prelingually deaf children. Its purpose is to demonstrate the often elementary nature of these difficulties. The effects: low educational and vocational attainment; social immaturity and poor world knowledge; demand that every possible effort is made to help the approximately one in a thousand people who suffer from prelingual deafness.

7

Chapter II The Computer-Assisted-Learning approach.

The rationale for using "language - understanding", computer-assisted-learning to help to improve the reading and writing abilities of deaf children is based upon psycholinguistic research into normal language acquisition. Many researchers believe that children are biologically predisposed to acquire language, and that linguistic competence results from interaction between this biological predisposition and the environment. (eg McNeill 1970). The linguistic environment of the developing child is therefore very important, but language acquisition is not something which happens passively. The learning of language is very much an active process. It is believed that hearing children discover the rules and concepts of language for themselves by a process of creative manipulation and hypothesis testing. Thus the diversity of both receptive and expressive linguistic experience is necessary for the acquisition and development of language. A child is an active agent of his own linguistic development. (eg Brennan 1976)

As there is no reason to suppose that the deaf child does not have the same biological or genetic predisposition to acquire language as the hearing child, the linguistic deficiency of the deaf child must be a result of disrupted environmental interaction. Obviously, in the first place, spoken linguistic input is disrupted and incomplete, but Bonvillian et al (1973) have pointed out that interaction is disupted in a second way.

Even if the child does succeed in formulating hypotheses to account for the regularities in the available input, he has difficulty in testing the hypotheses. Conversation with others, the means by which hearing children are able to obtain feedback by which their hypotheses may be tested, is also unsatisfactory. The deaf child both misunderstands and is misunderstood.

The aim of educators of the deaf, argues Brennan, should be to place deaf children in situations where they can manipulate language to form hypotheses, and where information about language structure is presented in a maximally assimiliable form. Although Brennan's case is chiefly against 'oralist' methods of educating the deaf, and in favour of 'total communication', Sewell et al (1979,1980) argue that computer-assisted-learning has the potential to meet the requirements of the ideal learning environment implied by Brennan. Sewell et al (1980) define these requirements as including that

a) " The child is involved in some degree of productive (rather than merely receptive) language use, in which language strings (sentences) can be produced and evaluated".

b) "Linguistic information is presented in meaningful contexts , rather than in isolation."

c) "There is immediate, accurate feedback and evaluation of response."

Sewell ee(1980) mention that a number of computer-assisted - learning programs have successfully been used with the deaf for teaching mathematics and as speech training aids. Also programs have been designed to teach written language (eg Sandalls 1976). Most of these programs involved time-sharing machines and the associated difficulties of expense, availability and response times, difficulties which may now be avoided by using mini and micro computers. However, a more important criticism of the language teaching programs is that "...the child is not nec-essarily involved in actively manipulating language and so, to a certain extent, remains a passive recipient."

Sewell et al therefore went on to develop an interactive program called JUMBLE in which the words and phrases are rearranged in an inappropriate order, and the user has to re-organize ~~recognize~~ the jumbled sentence into an acceptable grammatical form. The jumbled sentence appears on a video screen at the same time as a picture appears on a slide viewer. When correctly ordered the sentence describes some aspect of the picture. The slides act as aids to sematic context thus making the linguistic task more meaning-ful. Contextual aids may be very important in computer-assisted language learning. Gormley and Franzen (1978) have argued that in reading, semantic factors are far more important than syntactic ones. Clark and Sewell (1979) believe however that a combined syntactic and semantic approach is best.

JUMBLE seems to be an improvement on the more common drill-and-practice type of program because it contains an element of active linguistic manipulation. The linguistic task required of the learner involves both syntactic and semantic components, and it is a move towards the simulation of real life use of language. The sentences must be composed by the teacher and pre-stored in the computer. With careful preparation of the sentences the learning task can be directed towards those particular syntactic structures which are of greatest difficulty for the deaf, and these structures and the vocabulary used may be presented in a systematic or " analytical " way.[1] Preliminary results with JUMBLE are promising.

Bates et al (1979, 1980, 1981) have criticised programs which rely on sentences that have been pre-stored by the teacher because of their lack of versatility. They favour a generative approach to computer assisted language instruction. Their system, called ILIAD (Interactive Language Instructional Assistance for the Deaf) is a knowledge-based program that creates sentences for language instruction rather than presenting pre-stored material.

1. However, JUMBLE is not necessarily confined to analytical presentation and could be used by those educators who favour more natural teaching methods. Moores (1978) describes the two approaches.

This, they argue, can produce a limitless number of examples in which the vocabulary and syntactic complexity may be controlled by the learner. Also new vocabulary and material may easily be added without disturbing the *analytical " balance. It would be impossible to achieve this in a more conventional system because of the extensive storage and preparation required. The generative "core" of ILIAD is separate from the tutorial system and therefore a wider variety of tutorial purposes and a broader range of material are possible than with traditional systems.

A number of different exercises have been developed for use with ILIAD. For example, the system can ask the learner to correct a given sentence, to rewrite the sentence in its negative or plural form, to construct a 'Wh' question about a given sentence, or to expand the sentence by inserting given words.

Bates et al criticisms of traditional programs seem justified, and certainly few can offer such a wide range of exercises as ILIAD. Some of the ILIAD exercises would seem to require at least the same level of active linguistic manipulation as the JUMBLE program although other exercises would not. ILIAD at present lacks the aid to sematic context provided by JUMBLE's slides, but the addition of computer animated sequences is planned. This should enhance the purely syntactic dimension of many of the current exercises.

A possible criticism of ILIAD is that at its higher levels of syntactic complexity, it appears most suited to comparatively advanced requirements of learners of English as a foreign language, or remedial English students. Its effectiveness at the fundamental levels required by profoundly , prelingually deaf children remains to be shown. Nevertheless, it is an impressive piece of work.

Both JUMBLE and ILIAD, however, constrain the learner's
capacity to manipulate language creatively.   With JUMBLE the
sentence materials are provided beforehand by the teacher.
With ILIAD they are more various, being created by the computer
But in both programs, the words which the child may manipulate
are still fixed and, furthermore, there is only one right answer.
A closer simulation of normal linguistic interaction, and there
fore a closer simulation of the language learning process, would
be one in which the learner is free to create his own sentences.
Provided that the learner's efforts were properly directed, the
learner would then be able to creatively manipulate words to
form structures which could then be tested against the feedback
provided by the computer.   It would seem that this should ex-
pedite the development of linguistic competence.

To achieve this computationally, it is necessary for the program
to have the ability to analyse features of any sentence constructed by the learner, i.e. the program must have some language understanding capacity.   The program which is discussed
in this dissertation is therefore described as " language-
understanding".

Chapter 111. Considerations in designing a "language-understanding", computer-assisted-learning program.

111 a) Requirements.

In ILIAD the central part of the system, the sentence generator, is designed as a separate entity from the tutorial part of the system. This enables ILIAD to be used for different tutorial purposes and gives greater general versatility. This two component approach was adopted for LUCALD with, at this stage, an emphasis on developing the central analysis and feedback part of the system. The central part should be capable of analysing and giving feedback about the acceptability of any sentence constructed by the learner.

To achieve this the computer must first be able to recognise the learner's sentence as a sequence of words each consisting of a sequence of letters. It must then be able to determine whether the order of the words, i.e. the syntax of the sentence, is acceptable. Even if this is so the sentence may be nonsense or ambiguous. Therefore the program must also be able to determine the semantic acceptability of the learner's sentence. It is often difficult, sometimes impossible, for a human being to determine the meaning of a syntactically unacceptable sentence or of a sentence which contains unrecognisable letter sequences , i.e. mis-spelt or unknown words. This is considerably more difficult computationally. The simplest approach, therefore, is to perform the analysis of the learner's sentence in three stages: lexical, syntactic and semantic analysis.

IIIb) Operating restrictions

Computerised natural language processing[1] has yet to be fully
achieved. Some of the reasons for this are the syntactic and
semantic ambiguity of many common words, the infinite variety
of acceptable syntactic structures and the interdependence of
syntax and semantics.(Bundy et al 1978). These factors are
illustrated by the sentence "TIME FLIES LIKE AN ARROW" which
may be interpreted in four different way. (Raphael, 1976).
Limited language processing has been achieved only by defining
restrictions for the vocabulary, syntax and semantics on which
the computer operates. (eg Winograd 1972).

This was not seen as an insurmountable obstacle to the aims
of the project. Because the language problems of the deaf
are, as described in chapter 1, of a fundamental nature, it
was argued that a "language - understanding", computer-assisted-
learning program to teach reading and writing to deaf children
would not need to possess unrestricted language processing
abilities.

In defining the operating restrictions for LUCALD it was
necessary to have some idea of how the system might appear
during use. A JUMBLE-like configuration was envisaged, with
interaction taking place in writing on a video screen, and an
external picture providing the subject matter. Interaction
then has semantic, as well as syntactic dimensions. The
restrictions adopted are described in the following sections.

IIIc) Computer Hardware

In order to avoid the problems of time-sharing systems (expense, availability and response times), implementation should
be on a free-standing mini or micro computer. Furthermore,
the computer should be of a type likely to become widely

14   1 - see p. 22

available in schools. The aim must therefore be for micro computer implementation. Most artificial language-recognition programs have been implemented on large computers in very high level languages such as LISP. ILIAD, for example, has been under development in Inter Lisp on a DEC System 20 computer. Neither the language nor the system is likely to become common in schools in the near future. Hardware would therefore at first sight seem to be a major problem.

The system requirements of a "language-understanding" computer-assisted-learning program are mainly disk and string handling facilities. Disk seems necessary because it allows rapid access to large quantities of information which would exceed the internal storage space of a micro computer. String handling seems necessary because of the language manipulating require-ments of the program. Both facilities are available with the UCSD - Pascal Language and operating system which is now becoming available on the common micro computers. PASCAL also facilitates the careful structuring of the complex kind of program involved. The authors of ILIAD have recognised this and are now re-implementing using UCSD - Pascal on Apple and Cromemco systems. UCSD - Pascal was therefore chosen for LUCALD. However, it is convenient to have more powerful comput-ing facilities available during program development and there-fore LUCALD has been developed using UCSD - Pascal on an LSI-11 system. Transfer to a micro computer should eventually be possible.

III d) Lexical Analysis

On reading in the learner's sentence string, the program must first break down the string into a sequence of words and then determine whether each word is valid. The breakdown can be accomplished fairly easily using the UCSD - Pascal string handling commands, but word validation is more difficult. The

15

only practical method of validation is to refer to a list of
permitted vocabulary.   The size of the list may exceed internal storage space, so it is necessary to store it as an external
disk file.   This leads to the concept of a dictionary.

Having identified a word string, the program must determine
whether the string is entered in the dictionary. As a sequential dictionary search could result in unacceptably long program
response times, a faster method is necessary .   The UCSD
system supports direct access to disk files and therefore this
method was chosen.

The use of direct access demands that there is some method of
obtaining the dictionary file record number from the word string.
This may be achieved by using a hashing algorithm which transforms
the characters in the word string into numbers, and then performs
a sequence of arithmetical operations to produce a final figure
within a desired range.   The desired range is between 1 and
the number of records in the dictionary.   The disadvantage of
this method is that, in order to obtain entries evenly spread
throughout the dictionary, it is necessary to use algorithms
which order the entries unpredictably, i.e. the resulting file
is organised randomly.   There will also be a number of empty
records.   Sequential access to the file is therefore time con -
suming and some disk space is wasted.   However this is not a
problem at the lexical analysis stage where sequential access is
not required and processing speed is all important.

Following lexical analysis, the dictionary record number of each
word may be used to represent the actual character string. This
facilities processing because the program then has only to handle
integers and not variable length strings of characters.

111 e) Lexical Feedback.

There must be many possible ways of indicating that a particular word does not appear in the dictionary.   The question of the comparative effectiveness of alternative methods is one for experimental testing. The decision was made here to simply under-line the learner's word.

Frequently the reason for the absence of a learner's word from the dictionary will be that the learner has made a spelling error.   A possibly useful feedback device would be to suggest what the learner's target word might have been.

The spelling abilities of deaf children are surprisingly good. Hoeman et al (1976) found that 12 year old deaf children per-form as well as hearing children of the same age.   But whereas the mis-spellings of hearing children tend to sound the same as the target word, the mis-spellings of deaf children tend to have a similar written appearance to the target word,eg.'thristy ' for ' thirsty'.   This suggests that the words are stored and coded in the deaf child's brain as a visual sequence of letters.

Analysis of a sample of deaf childrens' spelling errors (Arnold and Crossley, 1981), showed that , as might be expected from the theory that deaf misspellings tend to be visual errors there were a number of visual consistences between the misspelt and intended words.   The initial letters were identical in 100% of the sample, the final letters in 64%, the second letters in 60% and the penultimate letters in 49% .   Single substitut-ions occurred in 24% of the sample and single transpositions in 22%.   Possible target words, if entered in the dictionary, may therefore be found by searching the dictionary for word strings which differ only in the above ways.   The actual methods chosen are described in chapter IV 6 d).   However, the method is not

17

foolproof, for example the targetword may not be entered in the dictionary at all, and therefore the learner must be given the option of rejecting the suggestion.

This method of extracting the learner's possible target word from the dictionary, requires that the dictionary is searched in a sequential way.   This is not practicable with the randomly organised structure of the dictionary.   A separate file in which the word strings are organised into groups of the same initial letter is required.   It should be possible to access the beginning of any group quickly.   An indexed-sequential organisation is most suitable to these requirements.   An indexed-sequential file, termed the spelling file, which is constructed from an analysis of the dictionary, was therefore designed.   This is much shorter in length than the dictionary because it does not need to contain the same amount of information, only the word strings being necessary, and there are no empty records.

111 f)   Syntax Analysis.

In order to determine the syntactic acceptability of a given sentence, it is necessary to have a definition of acceptable syntax.   It is obviously not possible to store a list of all acceptable sentences, therefore some rule based representation is required.   But because of the complex and inconsistent nature of natural syntax, it is probably impossible to define a set of rules which would include all acceptable sentences and exclude all unacceptable ones.   The learner must therefore be restricted to those syntactic forms which can be computationally represented.

Returning to the general levels of syntactic ability of deaf children, it is apparent that computational limitations would not prevent the construction of a program which could function

18

at a higher level and thus provide an aid to learning. This
could be done, for example, by using a context free phrase
structure grammar, i.e. a set of production rules which, when
applied in successive substitution, define the syntax of a
sentence. An algorithm is then required to parse the learner's
sentence with the phrase structure grammar, and a number of
different and rather complex ways of doing this are possible.
This approach is commonly adopted in compilers and often
described in that context, (eg Aho and Ulman 1977, Pollack 1972).
Another possible way to represent syntax is known as Transform-
ational Grammar. This is generally successful only when used
generatively (Raphael 1976) and is, in fact, the method used
by ILIAD. But a consideration of the requirements of deaf
children suggests a much simpler approach.

Educators of the deaf who take an "analytic" approach will
often set exercises on a particular syntactic structure. One
method known as LARSP (Language Assessment, Remediation and
Screening Procedure), (Crystal 1979) is a procedure for
identifying the linguistic characteristics of the disability
of an individual pupil and for suggesting guidelines for individual therapy. Another method involves the use of language
games which stress certain syntactic structures. Arnold and
Wildig (1981) point out that this allows a combination of the
close control of the "analytical" approach and the spontaneity
of the natural method. By designing an appropriate tutorial
component, LUCALD might be used to present language games.

It therefore seems that ᴧthe adoption of a computationally
complex, comprehensive syntactic representation, a simpler
and more limited representation is possible. The representation,
although limited to the requirements of one exercise or one
individual, should be interchangeable with other representations

19

in order that the program may be adapted to other purposes. This leads to the concept of a syntax file.

The syntax for LUCALD may now be represented by a finite-state-grammar. This is computationally the most straight forward means of imposing syntactic constraints on the recognition of sentences and has therefore been used in programs for automatic speech recognition. (eg Levinson and Liberman 1981). The grammar is represented by a network diagram which defines every possible sentence the program can recognise. Every path from the starting point of the diagram to the end point represents an acceptable sentence. Figure 1 shows a network diagram. Furthermore, the use of this method requires only a simple parsing algorithm. Recovery of parsing following an error in the learner's sentence, is also very easy to achieve.

Network diagrams may contain a separate node for each piece of vocabulary as in Levinson and Liberman (1981), in which case the diagram directly represents every possible sentence. A simpler diagram is obtained by defining the nodes so that each represents a set of words of a particular grammatical type. This allows vocabulary to be altered without changing the network structure. The simpler method was therefore selected. This requires that the grammatical function of each of the learner's words is known. The grammatical function of each word may be stored in the dictionary and read in during lexical analysis.

III q) Syntax feedback
As with lexical feedback, a simple approach was adopted at this stage of program development. It was decided to under-line any two words which are not permitted by the syntax file to occur successively. In the case of the first or final word

of the learner's sentence, only one word might need to be
underlined.

III h) Semantic Analysis

The domain of meaning in which interaction occurs between the
learner and the program, i.e. the vocabulary and semantic
restrictions, depend upon the picture. If an "analytic" approach
to the teaching of language is desired, the picture or pictures
should be selected so that only those items of vocabulary which
are of the required level are illustrated. The picture thus
determines the dictionary entries. It is also necessary to
restrict the semantic context in which each word may be used
so that all sentences describe the picture. Each word therefore needs an associated semantic representation, and it is
convenient to also store this in the dictionary.

There have been a number of different approaches to the representation of semantics. These are discussed, for example, by
Raphael (1976), Bundy (1978) and Pollack (1972) and include
predicate calculus, case grammars, conceptual dependency theory,
systemic grammar and augmented transition networks. There was
insufficient time to fully consider these alternatives, but a
method was devised in which words forming the semantic associates
of a given word could be included in the dictionary entry for
that word. For example the dictionary entry for "ON" might
contain "BOOK, TABLE" to indicate that a book is on a table.
This is described in chapter IV 5. Semantic acceptability
may then be determined by matching procedures.

III i) Semantic feedback

By adopting a three stage method of analysis, no syntactically
unacceptable sentence reaches semantic analysis. Any sentence
which has been found to be semantically unacceptable will be
syntactically correct. Semantic feedback may therefore be

achieved by manipulating the words in the learner's sentence string, inserting or removing negatives as necessary. This allows a range of appropriate semantic error messages to be returned.

1 : natural language processing – the language understanding
    abilities so far exclusively possessed by human
    information processors; this includes the ability to
    distinguish and to respond appropriately to all of
    the many language structures used in everyday
    written and spoken language.

Chapter IV - PROGRAM DESCRIPTION

24

IV 1 LUCALD

IV 1(a) Introduction

LUCALD consists of the following four programs:-

i MAINPROG   controls the interactive teaching process, but before this can proceed a syntax file, a dictionary and a spelling file must have been created by using the other three programs.

ii MAKESYNTAXFILE   creates the syntax file which represents a finite-state-grammar network diagram.

iii MAKEDICTIONARY   creates the dictionary and also the spelling file.

IV MAKESEMANTICS   controls semantic information which is stored in the dictionary.

The number of dictionaries and syntaxfiles is limited only by disk space. Different files may be created for different purposes. The teacher is asked to specify which dictionary and syntax file are to be used at the beginning of each run.

IV 1b) General description of the Interactive Process

The learner is required to construct a sentence and to type it at the console. The learner should attempt to construct a sentence which is within the syntax and domain of meaning described by the syntax file and dictionary specified for the current run.

LUCALD first searches the dictionary for each word appearing in the sentence. Any word which does not appear in the dictionary is underlined as a lexical error and the program then refers to the spelling file and makes suggestions about what the erroneous word should be. Another attempt to construct the sentence is then requested.

For **each** word which does appear in the dictionary, the program reads in its syntactic and semantic details. If there is no lexical error, i.e. all words of the sentence are entered in the dictionary, LUCALD parses the syntactic information obtained from the dictionary against the syntax file. Any part of the sentence which does not accord with the syntax file is under-lined as a syntax error, and a further attempt is requested.

Finally, if there is no syntactic error, the semantic inform-ation obtained from the dictionary is tested for inter-word consistency. If any test fails an appropriate message is given, eg "The horse is not black."

LUCALD is thus able to give feedback about the lexical, syntactic and semantic acceptability of a sentence composed by the learner. It does not at present provide a complete lesson. Work on the tutorial aspects of LUCALD remains to be done.

IV 2 THE SYNTAX FILE AND PROGRAM MAKESYNTAXFILE

IV 2(a) Introduction

The purpose of the syntax file is to represent the syntax of all acceptable sentences in a form which can be used by MAINPROG. A number of alternative syntax files may be constructed for different teaching purposes, and the one to be used during any MAINPROG run must be specified by the teacher at the beginning of the run. Syntax files are created by the program MAKESYNTAX-FILE and stored on the LUCALD disk. Each file represents a finite-state-grammar network diagram which must be constructed by the teacher before using the program MAKESYNTAXFILE.

IV 2(b) Preparation of the Network Diagram

In the network diagram, each node, excepting the first and the last, represents any one word of a particular 'syntax type' (eg noun-subject phrase-singular), the 'syntax type' being an integer equal to the node number. The paths from each node lead to nodes which indicate the permitted 'syntax types' of any words which follow. A syntactically acceptable sentence, therefore, consists of any sequence of words which have the 'syntax types' defined by the nodes in any path from the first (i.e. the start) node to the last (i.e. the end) node of the network. Figure 1 shows the network diagram for the syntax file PICTURES 1 SYNTAX.

There are some constraints which apply to the numbering of nodes.

i) The start node is always 0.

ii) All other nodes must be in the range 1 to max types, where maxtypes is a constant declared in all four programs.

iii) The terminal node must have a greater value than any other node.

iv) Every node number must be unique.

v) The numbering of the nodes must be consistent with the values 'syntax type' given to words by the dictionary.

vi) MAINPROG performs a number of arithmetic operations on 'syntax type' values. In order for this to occur there must be certain consistencies between node numbers representing words of the same grammatical type in different parts of the sentence. First, the 'syntax type' of a determiner, adjective or noun in the object phrase must be equal to the 'syntax type' of a determiner, adjective or noun in the subject phrase plus the MAINPROG constant 'objphrdiff' (object phrase difference). Secondly, the 'syntax type' of an adjective in the object phrase which qualifies a subject noun must be equal to that of an

27

Figure 1 : Network Diagram for PICTURES1 SYNTAX

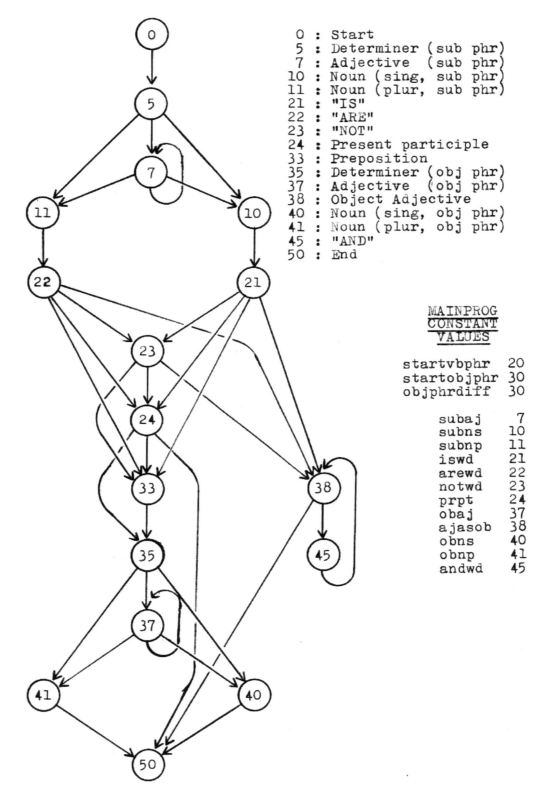

0 : Start
5 : Determiner (sub phr)
7 : Adjective (sub phr)
10 : Noun (sing, sub phr)
11 : Noun (plur, sub phr)
21 : "IS"
22 : "ARE"
23 : "NOT"
24 : Present participle
33 : Preposition
35 : Determiner (obj phr)
37 : Adjective (obj phr)
38 : Object Adjective
40 : Noun (sing, obj phr)
41 : Noun (plur, obj phr)
45 : "AND"
50 : End

MAINPROG
CONSTANT
VALUES

startvbphr	20
startobjphr	30
objphrdiff	30

subaj	7
subns	10
subnp	11
iswd	21
arewd	22
notwd	23
prpt	24
obaj	37
ajasob	38
obns	40
obnp	41
andwd	45

adjective in the object phrase which qualifies an object noun,
plus 1. In PICTURES1SYNTAX for example, objphrdiff = 30,
therefore an adjective, which in the dictionary has a 'syntax
type' value 7, may be converted to a value of 37 or 38 by
MAINPROG, depending on its position in the sentence. Thirdly,
it may be necessary to introduce further rules of this kind
for syntax diagrams more complex than PICTURES1SYNTAX.

vii) The node numbers of the subject, verb and object phrase
parts of the sentence must be within the ranges governed by
the MAINPROG constants 'startvbphr' and 'startobjphr'. In
PICTURES1SYNTAX these values are 20 and 30 respectively, thus
all subject phrase nodes be in the range 1 to 19, all verb
phrase nodes within 20 to 29, and all object phrase nodes
within 30 to 49. (49 being equal to the end node minus 1).
This is necessary in order that the arithmetic operations on
'syntax type' values be correctly performed by MAINPROG.

viii) In order that both syntactic and semantic analysis be
correctly carried out by MAINPROG, the node numbers must be
consistent with the 'syntax type' constants occurring in MAIN-
PROG and MAKESEMANTICS. Figure 1 lists these for PICTURES1SYN-
TAX. It can be seen that the above constraints involve all
files and programs. If a number of alternative syntax files
or dictionaries are used, it is obvious that the node numbering
method must be consistent throughout. Thus, for example, any
alternative syntax file to PICTURES1SYNTAX must, if it is to
be used with the same programs, use the value 10 for a singular
subject phrase noun.

IV 2c) Organisation of the Syntax File
Syntax files are organised and accessed sequentially. The
finite-state-grammar structure diagram is represented by a
series of integers each within the range 0 to maxtypes. The

29

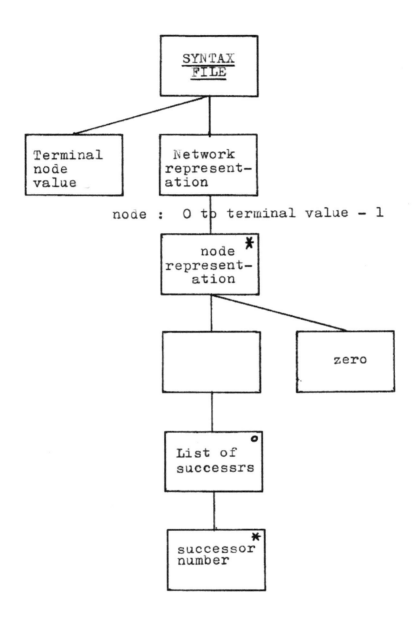

Figure 2 : The structure of the Syntax File

first integer is that of the terminal node number. Then, for each node from 0 to the terminal node minus 1, the file contains, in series, the values of all successor nodes, terminated by 0. The terminal node, of couse, has no successors. Figure 2 shows this structure diagrammatically.

IV 2d) Program MAKESYNTAXFILE

The program MAKESYNTAXFILE first requires the teacher to define the syntax file name and the identifying number of the terminal node of the network diagram. The teacher must then, for each node from 0 to the terminal node minus 1, enter the numbers of the successor nodes separated by spaces. If a node has no successors, eg because it not used in the diagram, then 0 must be entered. Finally, the syntax file is locked onto the LUCALD disk, and a permanent record is output to the line printer. MAKESYNTAXFILE requires thorough revision, possessing at present neither robustness nor interactive facilities for amending syntax files. Figure 3 shows the general structure of the program.

IV 3 THE DICTIONARY AND PROGRAM MAKEDICTIONARY

IV 3(a) Introduction

MAINPROG uses the information stored in the dictionary for lexical, syntactic and semantic analysis. The dictionary is first consulted to test the lexical acceptability of words used by the learner. If the learner's word appears in the dictionary then MAINPROG reads in the syntactic and semantic information associated with the word. As with syntax files, a number of alternative dictionaries may be constructed to accommodate different domains of meaning, and MAINPROG requires the dictionary to be used to be specified at the beginning of every run. Dictionaries are created by the program MAKEDICTIONARY

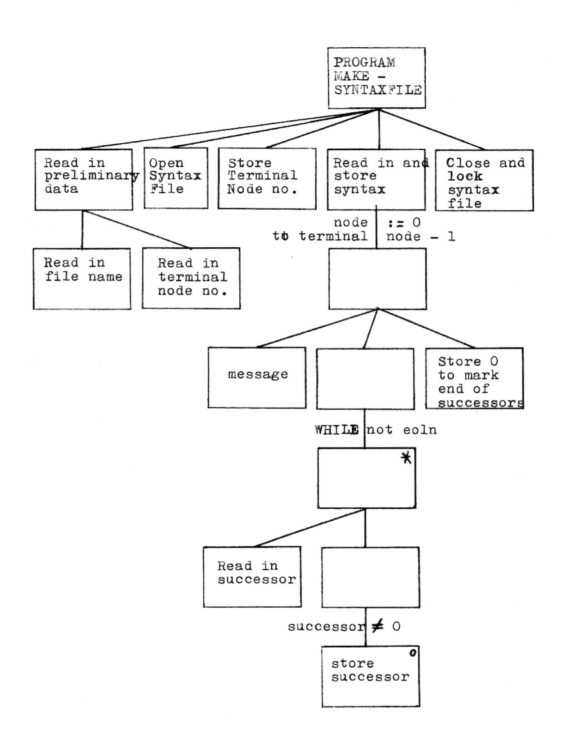

Figure 3 : Structure of Program MAKESYNTAXFILE

32

and stored on the LUCALD disk. Each dictionary consists of a list of vocabulary and the associated syntactic and semantic information for each word. The vocabulary and its syntactic information should be assembled by the teacher before using MAKEDICTIONARY. The semantic information is controlled by the program MAKESEMANTICS.

IV 3(b) Preparation of the vocabulary

The contents of the dictionary depends upon the domain of meaning in which the interaction between learner and program will occur. The dictionary should contain any vocabulary likely to be used by the learner. For example, if, as in the PICTURES 1 domain, the subject of the interaction is a picture or series of pictures, the teacher should attempt to include every word represented in the picture(s). Each word must then be given a 'syntax type' value. This should be the syntax file node number of the first possible occurrence of the word in the sentence. Thus in PICTURES1DICT all determiners have the 'syntax type' value 5. If the learner uses a determiner in its other possible position, at node 35, the 'syntax type' is altered during MAINPROG, although this alteration is not made to the dictionary file itself. For ease of insertion into the dictionary, words should be organised into groups of the same 'syntax type', eg all adjectives should be grouped together. It is not necessary to prepare semantic information at this stage.

IV 3(c) Organisation of the dictionary

The dictionary is organised randomly and accessed directly by use of a hashing algorithm. The number of records is defined by the constant 'maxwoods' which appears in all programs except MAKESYNTAXFILE. Usually many records will be empty. Each record contains the following fields:

1. A string of characters of length 0 to the constant 'max-length', each within the range 'A' to 'Z'. This is the word string.

2. The syntax type of the word; an integer within the range 0 (if record is empty) to 'maxtypes'.

3. An array of ten integers which represent semantic information: the semantic array. Some of these values will often be zero.

In an empty record there is a null string and all other values are zero. Figure 4 shows the structure of the dictionary diagrammatically.

IV 3(d) The Hashing Algorithm

Each word to be entered in the dictionary is transformed into an integer within the range 1 to maxwords, and this integer then represents the dictionary-file record number into which the word is entered. If the record so calculated is already occupied, the entry is made in the next available space in ascending record number order. If, in the search for the next available space, the end of the file (record number 'maxwords') is reached, the search resumes at record 1. The possibility of a full dictionary has not been covered by the present program which would, if this possibility was to occur, go into an infinite loop.

When the number of collisions (ie when two or more words have the same hash number) is low, this storage technique operates quickly. Recovery of information is also fast. If the number of collisions is high, then storage and recovery times increase. This method therefore is only efficient when the dictionary has at least 10% spare capacity (wirth p274). In this particular

Figure 4 : Structure of the Dictionary

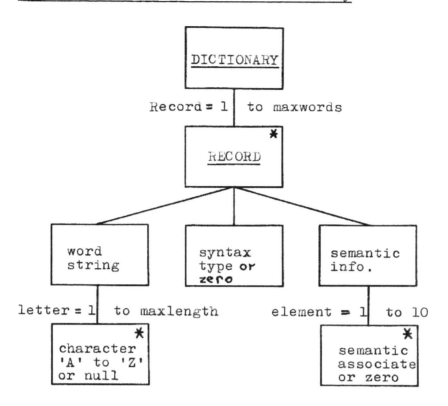

Figure 5 : Examples of the hashing transformation

in PICTURES1DICT (hashdiv = 2)

BLACK ──→ 453 + 540 = 993
993 mod 1000 = 993
993 div 2 = 496
Record number   496 + 1 = 497

AN ──→ 370
370 mod 1000 = 370
370 div 2 = 185
Record number   185 + 1 = 186

THROUGH──→ 412 + 859 + 100 = 1371
1371 mod 1000 = 371
371 div 2 = 185
Record number   185 + 1 = 186
Record 186 already occupied by "AN"
Record number 187 is empty
Record number = 187

35

application, where feedback times are of greater importance than disk storage space, spare capacities of over 50% are probably not unacceptable.

The hashing technique has also a second important advantage. Each word may be represented by its dictionary record number . This allows the program MAINPROG to operate in a more efficient manner, using integers rather than variable-length strings of characters.

The algorithm used is based on the Williams algorithm(Williams 1959). This has the effect that the integers calculated from any number of word strings will be evenly distributed through-out the required range, thus minimising collisions.

The algorithm is as follows: Each letter of the word is trans-formed into an integer within the range 1 to 9. This is done by manipulating the internal ASCII representation of each char-acter. The results of this operation may be seen in figure 6. These integers are then multiplied and added in groups of three as follows until the end of the word is reached. The first integer in each group is multiplied by 100 and added to the second integer multiplied by 10. The third integer is added unchanged. The process then starts again with the addition of the fourth integer multiplied by 100. This continues until the last integer has been added to the running total (after having been multiplied by 100, 10 or 1). The modulus of the running total by 1000, and then by the constant "hashdiv ' is calculated.

The number is finally brought into the required range by adding 1. In PICTURES 1 DICT, maxwords=500,therefore hashdiv = 2. The final value calculated from any word string will be within

36

the range 1 to 500. Figure 5 shows some examples of
the whole calculation.

Figure 6 : Transformation of characters to integers

Character			Integer
H	Q	Z	1
I	R		2
A	J	S	3
B	K	T	4
C	L	U	5
D	M	V	6
E	N	W	7
F	O	X	8
G	P	Y	9

IV 3(e) Program MAKEDICTIONARY

In operation, MAKEDICTIONARY offers the following menu selection:-

    0 Create new blank dictionary.

    1 Add to an existing dictionary.

    2 Query and/or amend an existing dictionary.

    3 Display or print dictionary.

    4 Update spelling error file.

    5 End program

0 Create new blank dictionary:

When the teacher wishes to create a completely new dictionary an empty dictionary must first be made by using this option. The teacher is required to name the new file, and then a file of empty records is stored on the LUCALD disk. The file is 'maxwords' records long. Selection 2 or 3 must then be used to make entries in the dictionary.

1 Add to an existing dictionary:

By selecting this option, a large number of words may quickly be entered in any existing dictionary, in groups of the same 'syntax type'. If the dictionary file name has not previously been specified in the current program run, the user is first required to do so.

To enter a group of words, the user must first specify the 'syntax type' of the group and then may enter words, so long as there remains space in the dictionary, simply by typing them in. If at any time a word which already exists in the diction- ary is entered, the old entry is overwritten and the user warned. To end the sequence a blank should be entered. The user is then offered the choice of entering another group of words or of returning to the menu.

2 Query and/or amend an existing dictionary:

This option may be used to examine any dictionary entry. If
the dictionary file name has not beenspecified in the current
program run the user is first required to do so. The user
may then enter the queried word. If the word is not entered
in the dictionary, a message to this effect appears, otherwise
the entry and 'syntax type' are displayed. The user may also
examine but not alter the semantic information field. The
user then has the option of altering or deleting the record.

Menu Selection 2 is dangerous, at present, because it is
possible for the user to alter a word string so that it is out
of hash position in the dictionary, and therefore inaccessible.
The program should be altered so that if the spelling of a
word is altered, it becomes entered in the dictionary at its
correct record number, and not at the position of the word it
replaced.

3 Display or print dictionary:

This may be used to display on the screen or to print out the
whole or just part (ie one syntax type) of the dictionary. The
user names the dictionary file if this has not been done already,
selects the required place and extent of display and then
receives the display with additional information about the
total number of entries in the dictionary. Program MAKESEMANTICS
contains this same display or print procedure.

4 Update spelling file:

This is covered in the next main section.

5 End/Program:

This allows the user to escape the program. This is not per-

39

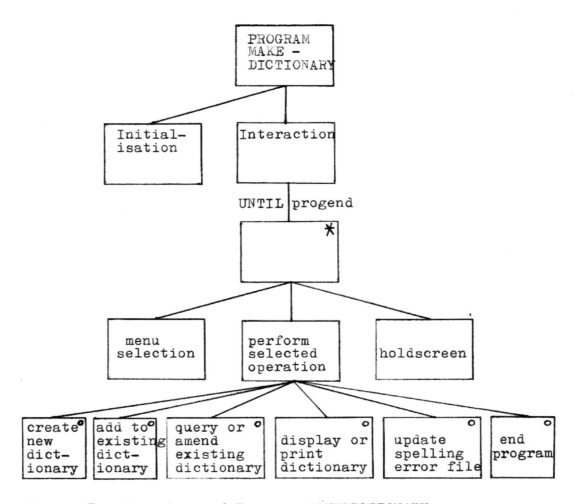

Figure 7 : Structure of Program MAKEDICTIONARY

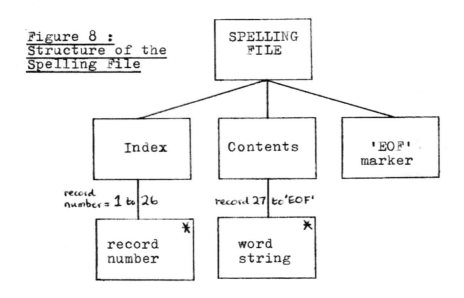

mitted if during the current run the dictionary has been amended without subsequently updating the spelling file.

Figure 7 shows the general structure of program MAKEDICTIONARY.

IV 4 THE SPELLING FILE

IV 4(a) Introduction

The spelling file provides a means by which MAINPROG can make suggestions about words used by the learner which do not appear in the dictionary. If the contents of the dictionary are comprehensive, this procedure should only be necessary when the learner has made a spelling error. A spelling file, separate from the dictionary, is needed because the organisation of the dictionary does not facilitate the access of words with a particular initial letter; the basis of the spelling suggestion procedure. The spelling file is controlled by menu selection 4 of program MAKEDICTIONARY. The name of the spelling file is always equal to that of its associated dictionary with the prefix 'S', truncated if necessary to a length of 15 characters. The file requires no prior preparation by the teacher.

IV 4(b) Organisation of the Spelling File

The spelling file has an indexed-sequential ogranisation. Records 1 to 26 form the index and the remaining records each contain one entry. Each entry is a string of characters equal to one of the word strings in the dictionary. There is one spelling file entry for every non-empty dictionary record. There are no empty records in the spelling file.

Spelling file entries are grouped by initial letter. Each of the 26 index records contains an integer equal to the record number at which a group of entries begins. Thus index record 1 contains the value 27, being the number of the record cont-

aining the first of any entries with the initial letter 'A'.
The final record of the file contains the string 'EOF'. The
reason for this will be explained in the next section. Figure
8 shows the organisation of the spelling file diagrammatically.

IV 4(c) Updating the Spelling File

The spelling file must be updated by selecting option 4 of
program MAKEDICTIONARY whenever any additions, deletions or
alterations have been made to the word strings in the dictionary.
The program cannot be ended until the spelling file has been
updated.

Updating occurs as follows: The dictionary is analysed in
order to obtain a count of the number of word strings beginning
with each initial letter, and also the number of entries in
total. If a spelling file already exists for the dictionary it
is then reopened, otherwise a new file is begun. In either
case the spelling file is then initialised by entering the
analysis data in the index, and by creating the required number
of empty records. Thus any pre-existing spelling file is overwritten. The entry 'EOF' is then made in the final record.
The dictionary is then read serially, and the word string from
each non-blank record is entered in the first available appropriate space in the spelling file. The entries in each spelling
file group are therefore entered in the same order as they
appear in the dictionary, not in any alphabetical order beyond
that of the initial letter.

During the initialisation phase of this process, it is possible
that not all of the previous spelling file entries are emptied.
This could occur after deletions have been made in the dictionary. The old spelling file will therefore be longer than the
new, and the end of the old file will still exist. It is for

this reason that the string 'EOF' is added in a record at the end of the file.

IV 5 THE SEMANTIC ARRAY AND PROGRAM MAKESEMANTICS

IV 5(a) Introduction

Each word record in the dictionary contains an array in which semantic information may be stored. This is used by MAINPROG to determine the semantic acceptability of sentences. The contents of the array are controlled by program MAKESEMANTICS, but before any information can be inserted it is necessary that the teacher performs a semantic analysis of the domain of meaning through which the interaction between learner and program takes place.

IV 5(b) Preparation of semantic information

The semantic information required consists of a list of certain relationships between the words occurring in the domain of meaning. The list should be as comprehensive as possible. Distinction must be made between relationships which are possible and and relationships which are represented in the domain, i.e. the difference between 'can' and 'does'. The semantic information required is that which is actually represented.

For the PICTURES1 domain, using the PICTURES1SYNTAX, the following details were found to be necessary.

i) For every adjective, a list of nouns to which they apply.

ii) For every preposition, a paired list of subject and object nouns.

iii) For every present participle, a paired list of subject and object nouns.

iv) For every present participle it was necessary to know whether a preposition in the object phrase was mandatory, optional

43

or prohibited when an object phrase was present in the sentence. This analysis should apply only to usage of the present participle within the domain of meaning being used, not to general usage.

v) Where synonyms occur, one synonym must be selected as the master, and this used in all the above analyses. For each slave synonym a note of its master must be made.

These details, stored in the semantic arrays, allowed MAINPROG to make a number of tests for semantic acceptability. The introduction of further semantic tests to MAINPROG and further semantic information to the arrays would allow more sophisticaed interaction to occur.   Chapter IV 7, gives an example of the vocabularyand semantic information for one of the PICTURES 1 items.

IV 5 (c) Program MAKESMANTICS is similar to that of MAKEDICTION- ARY in that it offers an interactive menu selection. Ideally the two programs should be combined. MAKESEMANTICS offers the following menu :-

1. Query and/or amend the semantic array of any record in an existing dictionary

2. Display or print dictionary

3. End program.

The important part of this program is Option 1. Options 2 and 3 have similar functions to options 3 and 5 of program MAKE- DICTIONARY and will not be described again. One difference is that there is no need to update the spelling file before ending program MAKESEMANTICS.   Figure 9 shows the general structure of the program.

At present the space available in the dictionary for semantic information is limited to an array of ten integers. This forms

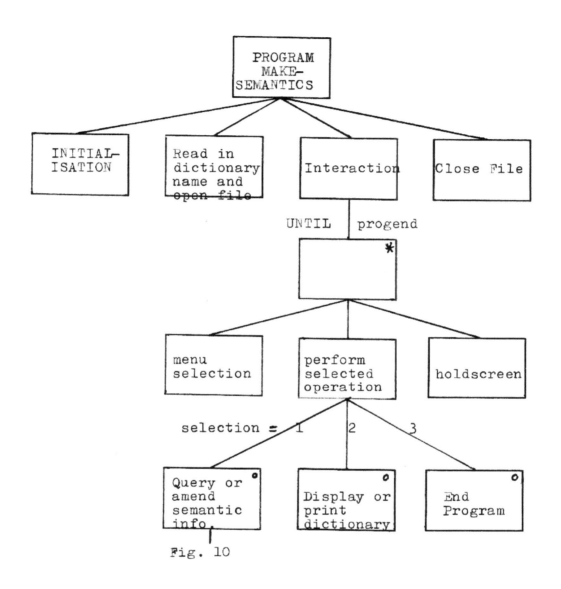

Fig. 10

Figure 9 : General Structure of Program MAKESEMANTICS

the third field of each record. The integers are equal in value
to the dictionary record numbers of other dictionary entries,i.e.
the entries for semantically associated words.

After selecting option 1, the user is first required to enter
the dictionary name if this has not already been done during the
current program run. The user may then state the queried entry,
and if this is not entered in the dictionary a message to this
effect appears. If the queried word does appear in the dictionary then the record is displayed on the screen. MAKESEMANTICS
refers to the dictionary to obtain the full word strings of the
records numbered in the semantic array. These are also displayed. If one or more of the semantic array values is zero,
then the fact that this call is empty is displayed instead of a
word string. To alter any of the semantic values, the user must
enter the cell number (1 to 10) followed by the word string of
the new semantic associate. MAKESEMANTICS ensures that there is
a dictionary entry for the new associate, and if so, enters the
record number in the appropriate cell of the semantic array.
If the new semantic associate is not entered in the dictionary,
then its use is not permitted. Finally, the user may alter
another semantic cell or return to the menu. The structure of
this menu selection is shown in figure 10.

Semantic array cell 10 is different, being used for semantic
rules. Rules are represented by negative integers which may be
inserted direct. This is described in d).

IV5 d) Contents of the Semantic Array.

The information obtained during the procedure described in b)
above, may be inserted into the semantic array using program
MAKESEMANTICS as described in c) above, MAINPROG reads in and
makes comparisons between the semantic arrays of the words used

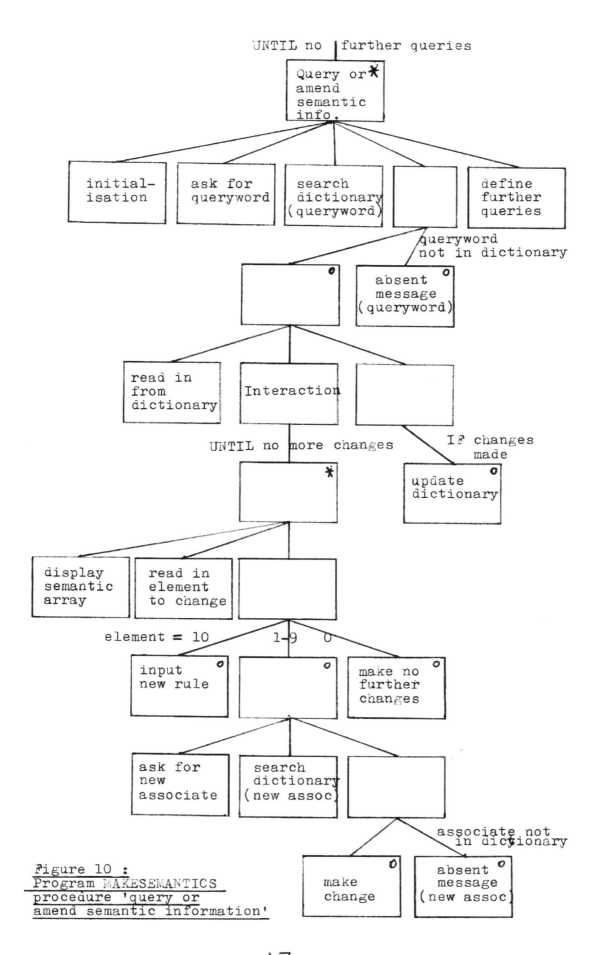

Figure 10 :
Program MAKESEMANTICS
procedure 'query or
amend semantic information'

47

in the learner's sentence. These comparisons are made in a number of tests which have been developed in conjunction with PICTURES1SYNTAX, PICTURES1DICTIONARY and the PICTURES1 domain. The tests require that the information is entered in the array in a certain way, and this is shown in figure 11. Semantic array cells 1 to 8 are used in a different way from 9 and 10.

i) Semantic array cells 1 to 8.

For each adjective, one noun to which the adjective applies, is entered in each cell. Some or all cells may be empty.

For each present participle, a pair of subject and object nouns is inserted in cells 1 and 2, 3 and 4, 5 and 6 or 7 and 8. Some or all the cell pairs may be empty.

Preposition arrays also contain subject and object noun pairs in exactly the same arrangement as present participles.

For all other grammatical types cells 1 to 8 are empty.

ii) Semantic cell 9

Semantic cell 9 contains the record number of the record's own semantic meaning. In PICTURES1DICTIONARY this, for all words other than nouns, and in fact for most nouns, is the same as the record's own number. Program MAKEDICTIONARY automatically inserts the record's own number into cell 9, and it must be intentionally altered if it is to be different. Cell 9 should not contain the record's own number in the case of a noun which is not a master synonym. This is best illustrated by example. In the PICTURES1 domain there is one representation which might be referred to be any of the synonyms LADY, WOMAN or MOTHER. The word LADY was chosen as the master, and this was used in the semantic fields of associated words, eg in one of the semantic cells of FAT and in one of the subject noun

48

Figure 11 : Use of semantic array in PICTURES1DICTIONARY

Element	Adjective	Noun	Present Participle	Preposit[n]	Other
1	Noun rec number or empty	E	Subject noun rec number or empty	Subject noun rec number or empty	E
2	-do-	E	——paired—— Object noun rec number or empty	——paired—— Object noun rec number or empty	E
3	-do-	E	as 1	as 1	E
4	-do-	E	—— pair —— and 2	——pair—— and 2	E
5	-do-	E	as 1	as 1	E
6	-do-	E	——pair—— and 2	——pair—— and 2	E
7	-do-	E	as 1	as 1	E
8	-do-	E	—— pair —— and 2	——pair—— and 2	E
9	own rec number	If master then own rec no else master rec no	Own rec number	Own rec number	Own rec number
10	E	E	-1 mndtory -2 prohib -3 optionl	E	E

E = empty element (zero)

49

semantic cells of PUSHING. WOMAN and MOTHER are 'slave' synonyms, and in order that the semantic tests in MAINPROG may
operate correctly, their semantic array cells 9 should contain,
not their own record numbers, but the record number of their
master synonym LADY.

iii) Semantic cell 10.

This is used to represent semantic rules. In the PICTURES1
domain only one has so far been introduced. This is used with
present participles, therefore for all other grammatical types
cell 10 has the value 0. Negative integers are used to represent
semantic rules. The rules represent the information obtained
in section b)iv) above. The value -1 is used when a preposition
is mandatory, -2 when prohibited and -3 when optional.

It is certain that the development of syntax files and domains
other than PICTURES1 will require that additional rules and
additional semantic information be recorded. The above approach
reflects only the work done so far on the PICTURES1 domain.

IV 6 MAINPROG

The general appearance of MAINPROG during operation has been
described in section IV 1(b). Here the operation of the program
will be described in terms of data operations. Fig 14 shows the
general structure.
(p.64)
IV 6(a) Main data structures

There are two main data structures, the syntax, which remains
unchanged for the duration of each run, and the sentence, which
changes at each interaction.

i) Internal syntax representation.

At the beginning of each run, the external syntax file is read
in and stored internally. The internal storage is as follows.
For each node from 0 to maxtypes, where maxtypes is a constant

Figure 12 : Internal storage of syntax
(Part of PICTURES1SYNTAX)

Array of base addresses   Linked list of records

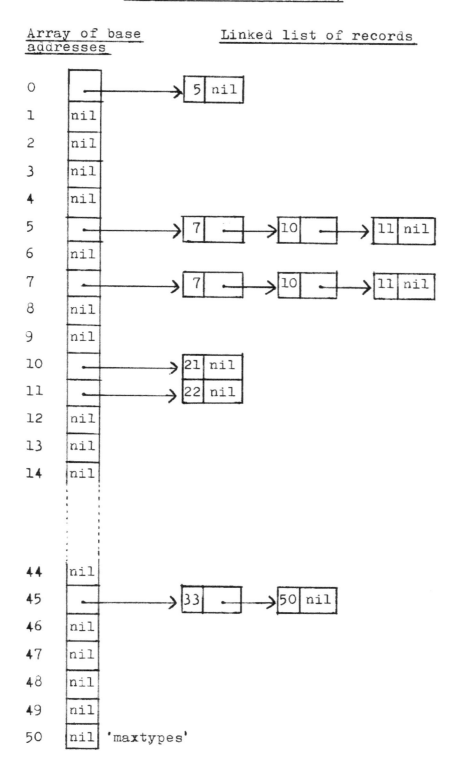

which represents the maximum number of nodes allowed, as
described in IV 2(b), there exists a linked list of records.
Each record contains, firstly, the node number of a successor
and, secondly, the address of the record containing the number
of the next successor. The second field of the final record
in each list contains a nil address. The number of records in
each list is therefore equal to the number of successors of the
node to which the list applies. The address of the first record
in each list, the base address, is stored in an array of length
0 to maxtypes. If any node number in this range is unused,
i.e. there exists no node of a particular number in the syntax
network diagram, the value stored in the array of base addresses
is nil, and the number of records in the linked list is zero.
Figure 12 shows this in a diagrammatic representation of part
of PICTURES1SYNTAX.

ii) Internal representation of the sentence.
The sentence is stored word by word in an array of 'word'
records. The array is emptied at the start of each interaction.
The size of the array is governed by the constant 'maxsent'
(maximum sentence length). Although this structure restricts
the number of words a sentence may contain and is wasteful of
internal storage space when sentences are short, it allows the
elements of the array to be accessed directly, and thus allows
MAINPROG to operate more quickly than would a dynamic storage
structure. Each word record contains, in addition to the word
string itself, a number of other fields. There are seven fields
in all. These are:-

1. The syntax type. An integer in the range 0 to maxtypes - 1.

2. The dictionary record number. An interger in the
   range 0 to maxwords.

52

3. The word string. A string of characters, each within the range 'A' to 'Z', of length maxlength.

4. Semantic data. An array of ten integers equal to the ten elements of the semantic field of the dictionary entry.

5. Start position. The position of the first character of the word string in the sentence line typed by the learner.

6. Word length. The number of   characters in the word string.

7. Error mark. An integer in the range 0 to 20 indicating whether this word in the sentence is in error, and if so, what the nature of the error is. Figure tabulates the use of this field.

At each interaction the learner's sentence is read in as a string of 80 characters. Within the string, each group of adjacent capital letters, i.e. within the range 'A' to 'Z' is transferred into field 3 of consecutive elements of the sentence data structure. All other characters are regarded as spaces. The upper case lock key of the console should therefore be depressed throughout any run of MAINPROG. Also at this stage, fields 5 and 6 of each word record are defined. All unused fields and all unused elements of the sentence array remain as initialised, with a null string in field 3, and zero in all other fields.

If, when copying sub strings from the sentence line to the word records, there are found more than 'maxlength' adjacent capital letters, then only the first maxlength characters are copied, and field 7, errormark, is set to 2.

Figure 13 : Use of the word record error mark

```
0        initial value
1        no error
2        lexical error - word not in dictionary
3                      - word too long
4        syntactic error - adjacent words error
5                        - sentence not correctly started
6                        - sentence not correctly ended
7 - 9    unused
10       semantic error - subject adjective
11                      - object adjective
12                      - subject adjective in object phr.
13                      - preposition
14                      - present participle
15                      - object noun and present partic.
16                      - subject noun and present partic.
17                      - preposition missing
18-20 unused
```

IV 6(b) Lexical Analysis

The dictionary is searched for each string occupying field 3 of a record in the sentence array. This is achieved by using the same hashing algorithm and procedure as used in MAKE-DICTIONARY. The search therefore finds in the dictionary either a string equal to the one in the sentence array, in which case the word is lexically correct, or an empty diction-ary record, in which case a lexical error has occurred.

If the word is lexically correct, then fields 1,2 and 4 of the word record in the sentence array are copied from the dic-tionary, and field 7 is set to 1. If the word is lexically in error, the seventh field of the word record is set to 3.

IV 6(c) Lexical Feedback

For each non-empty word record in the sentence array. If the errormark is other than zero then, by referring to the fifth and sixth fields of the word record, the appropriate part of the sentence typed by the learner is underlined. If the errormark is equal to 2 the message 'WORDTOOLONG' is included in the underline. The global variable 'lexerror' is set to true and this prevents syntactic and semantic analysis from taking place.

IV 6(d) Suggest-Word

If one or more of the learner's words are not entered in the dictionary then suggestions are made as to what each erroneous word should have been. When the reason for the learner's word being absent is that the learner has made a spelling error, then this procedure gives useful feedback. If, however, the learner has correctly spelt a word which is absent from the dictionary because of oversight or because of its low frequency of occurence, then this procedure gives a type of false feedback. Care in preparation of the vocabulary is therefore essential.

Suggest-word operates by comparing the learner's word with the strings in the spelling file which commence with the same character. The first of these spelling file strings is assessed by referring to the appropriate spelling file index record. The remaining relevant strings are then searched serially. If there are no spelling file strings which commence with the same character as the learner's word string, then the record to which the index points contains a string of different initial character.

Suggestword applies a number of tests of similarity to the learner's word string and to each spelling file string of the same initial character. If a test is successful then the spelling file string is displayed on the screen as a suggestion. The tests are grouped into four levels. The relevant spelling file strings are tested once at each level. If there are no successful tests at levels 1,2 or 3 then the next level of tests commences. At the end of levels 1,2 and 3, if suggestions have been made, the learner is asked to accept or reject the suggestions. All level four suggestions are automatically accepted. If the suggestions are rejected then the next level of tests commences. If the suggestions are accepted then suggestions concerning the next erroneous word in the sentence will begin, or, if none, the learner will be asked to attempt the sentence again.

The rationale behind the tests is described in chapter III. The tests are as follows:

Level 1
The spelling file string is suggested when

i) the first four characters are equal to those of the learner's word string. This test is made only if both strings are longer than 3 characters and are of different lengths.

ii) the strings are of equal length and of only one character difference.

iii) the strings are of equal length and contain the same characters in different order. This test operates by summing the internal ASCII representation of the characters and may therefore not always operate as intended.

Level 2

The spelling file string is suggested when

i) the first three characters are equal to those of the learner's word string

or ii) the first two and the last characters are equal to those of the learner's word string.

These tests are made only if both strings are either longer than three characters, or longer than two characters and of different lengths.

Level 3

The spelling file string is suggested when the first two characters are equal to those of the learner's word string. This test is made only when both strings are longer than one character.

Level 4

All spelling file strings with the same initial character as that of the learner's word string are suggested. If there are none then a message to this effect is displayed.

At present, strings which have been suggested and rejected by the learner may be suggested again at subsequent level of testing, and will certainly be suggested again at level 4.

IV 6(e) Syntax Analysis

In syntax analysis, MAINPROG parses the syntactic information in field 1 of each non-blank word record of the sentence array, with the internal syntax representatio   This proceeds in the following way. The program compares the 'syntax type' of the first word record with the first successor of node 0 (i.e. the entry in the first field of the record pointed to by the address stored in element 0 of the array of base addresses). If the two integers differ, the program repeatedly accesses the next record in the linked list of successors until either the end of the list is reached, or the two integers are equal. If the end of the list has been reached then a syntax error has occurred - the learner's first word not being of a permitted 'syntax type' for a word in this position. If, alternatively, the 'syntax type' of the learner's first word does equal one of the successors of node 0 then the word is syntactically acceptable. Following syntactic acceptance, the program accesses the list of successors of the 'syntax type' of the accepted word, and compares each entry in this list with the 'syntax type' of the following word of the sentence. The following word may then be syntactically accepted or rejected. Provided that every word is accepted, this process continues to the last word of the sentence. Provided, then, that the sentence has been properly completed, the terminal node of the syntax will be equal to one of the successors of the 'syntax type' of the final word.

When a syntactic error has occurred the program may still
continue as above. However, following a syntax error, the
error mark of the erroneous word record (field 7) in the
sentence array is set to 4, as is the error mark of the
preceding word. There are two exceptions to this. When the
first word of the sentence is not acceptable as a first word
then the errormark is set to 5 and there is no preceding error
mark to adjust. When the last word of the sentence is not
acceptable as a last word then the errormark is set to 6.
Although this information is not used in the present program
to give differential syntax error feedback, all words with
syntax errors being underlined in the same way, differential
feedback is possible. Also after a syntax error the global
variable 'synerror' is set to true to prevent semantic analysis
from proceeding. Underlining of syntax errors occurs in a
similar way to that of lexical errors. In addition a syntax
error message is displayed.

Syntactic analysis contains one further procedure. This is
necessary because the 'syntax type' values of field 1 of each
word record have been copied direct from the dictionary. As
mentioned in sections IV 2(b) and IV 3(b) this is not necessarily correct because the same word may be used in different
parts of the sentence. As each word of the sentence is accessed,
syntax analysis performs any necessary **arithmethical** operation
on the syntax type and alters field 1 of the record in the
sentence array. The 'syntax types' of any words following the
start of the verb phrase, which are less than the constant
'startvbphr', are altered by the addition of the constant
'objphrdiff'. Thus in PICTURES1SYNTAX the value of the 'syntax
type' of determiners which occur in the object phrase are
altered from 5, by 30, to 35. Adjectives in the object phrase
which refer to the subject noun, in addition to being altered

as above, are also altered by the addition of 1, eg to 38 in
PICTURES1SYNTAX.

IV 6(f) Semantic Analysis

Semantic analysis is performed by a number of tests of
consistency between the values contained in the ten-element
semantic array which has been copied from the dictionary for
each word of the sentence, and which forms field 4 of each
word record in the sentence array. The analysis occurs in two
stages. First all the non-blank records of the sentence array
are passed to i) discover whether certain grammatical structures are used in the sentence, and ii) to obtain the positions
(ie the word order number or sentence array element) of certain
sentence components. Secondly, depending upon which structures
are present, the appropriate semantic tests are performed.

For PICTURES1 domain using PICTURES1DICT and PICTURES1SYNTAX
the following information is required and tests performed.

Information required: i) whether the sentence contains or
does not contain a negative; an object; a subject adjective;
an object adjective; an object adjective which relates to the
subject noun; a present participle; a preposition. This
information is recorded in a series of boolean variables.
ii) the position in the sentence of the subject noun; the
object noun (if any); the present participle (if any); the
preposition (if any). This information is stored in variables
of type integer within the sub range 0 to 'maxsent'.

Tests performed:

i) the adjective-noun tests. This tests whether the value
    of semantic element 9 of a noun, is equal to one of the
    values of semantic elements 1 to 8 of an adjective.

ii) subject test. This tests whether the value of semantic

element 9 of a subject noun is equal to one of the values of semantic elements 1,3,5 or 7 of a present participle, a preposition or any other word type which relates to the subject noun.

iii) object test. This tests whether the value of semantic element 9 of an object noun is equal to the value contained in the semantic element plus 1 of a present participle, a preposition or any other word type which returned a successful subject test.

These tests are used as follows:

i) For each subject adjective, each object adjective relating to the object noun and each object adjective relating to the subject noun, the adjective test is used upon the semantic information of the adjective and the appropriate noun.

ii) If the sentence contains a preposition, the subject test is performed upon the semantic information of the subject noun and that of the preposition, and the object test upon the semantic information of the object noun and that of the preposition.

iii) If the sentence contains a present participle, the subject and object tests are used in a similar way to ii) above, except that no object test is performed if no object noun is present.

iv) If the sentence contains a present participle then semantic element 10 of the present participle stipulates whether a preposition is mandatory, prohibited or optional in the sentence. The presence or absence of a preposition in the sentence is tested accordingly.

61

Semantic feedback is provided by manipulating the words of
the learner's sentence and re-displaying them on the screen.
These manipulations are as follows:-

i)   The adjective error message which displays
     "THE (noun) IS NOT (adjective)."
     When the sentence is negative and the adjective occurs in
     the object phrase but relates to the subject noun, then
     "NOT" is omitted.

ii) The negative sentence which rewrites the learner's sentence,
     omitting adjectives, and inserting "NOT" after the verb.
     If the learner's sentence is negative then "NOT" is
     removed.

iii) The verb-preposition error message which informs the
     learner that the verb-preposition combination he has used
     is not allowed.

iv) The absent preposition error message which re-displays
     the learner's sentence, omitting adjectives, and inserting
     "?????" at the point of the missing preposition.

v)   The subject-verb negation which re-displays the subject
     and verb phrases used by the learner, inserting "NOT"
     after the verb. If the learner's sentence is negative
     then "NOT" is removed.

Semantic feedback is given when one or more of the semantic
tests fails. A failed adjective-noun test results in an
adjective error message except where the learner has nega-
tively but correctly stated that an adjective used in the
object phrase does "not" relate to the subject noun. A failed
subject test results in a subject-verb negation if the test
was performed using a present participle, or a negative
sentence if the test was performed using a preposition. Again

62

this does not occur when the sentence is negative. A failed
object test results in a negative sentence. The use of the
other error messages is self explanatory.

At present, when a sentence contains more than one error, then
when two or more errors result in the same message, that
message will be displayed two or more times.

Semantic errors are also reflected in adjustments to the error
mark in the word records. See figure 13 for details of this.

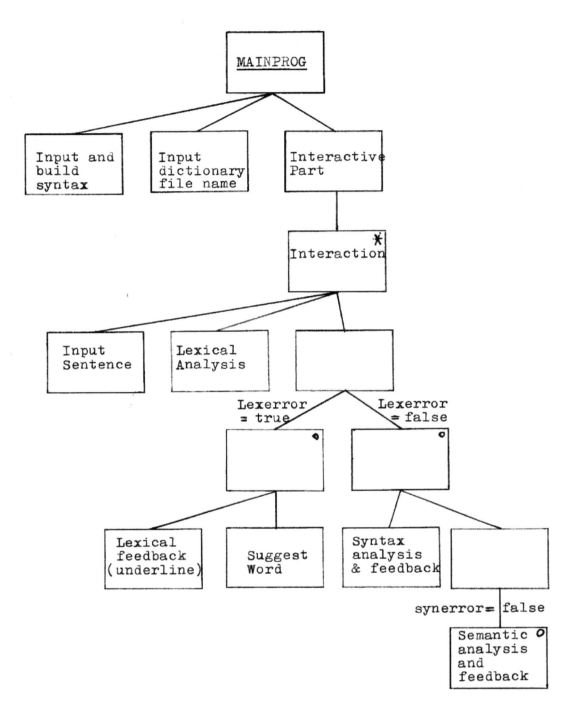

Figure 14 : General Structure of MAINPROG

64

IV 7 THE PICTURES1 DOMAIN

During program development PICTURES1SYNTAX and PICTURES1-DICTIONARY were constructed for testing and demonstration purposes. The PICTURES1 domain uses a number of line drawings taken from the sentence Comprehension Test (Wheldall et al, 1979) and semantically enriched with colour. (Fig. 15). The network diagram for the syntax was constructed to include most of the structures used in the (Fig 1) stimulus sentences of the test.

The dictionary contains the following vocabulary and semantic information relating to picture 4.

Word	Syntax type	Semantic information				
		1	2	3	------ 9	10
Red	7	Pram				Red
Pram	10					Pram
Big	7	Lady				Big
Fat	7	Lady				Fat
Woman	10					Lady
Lady	10					Lady
Mother	10					Lady
Pushing	24	Lady	Pram			Pushing -2
Walking	24	Lady	Pram			Walking -1
With	33	Lady	Pram			With

In preparing the PICTURES1 domain little attention has been paid to the 'analytical' aspects of the material. Neither the syntax nor the vocabulary is graded.

Fig 15   THE PICTURES 1 DOMAIN
(from Wheldall et al, 1979)

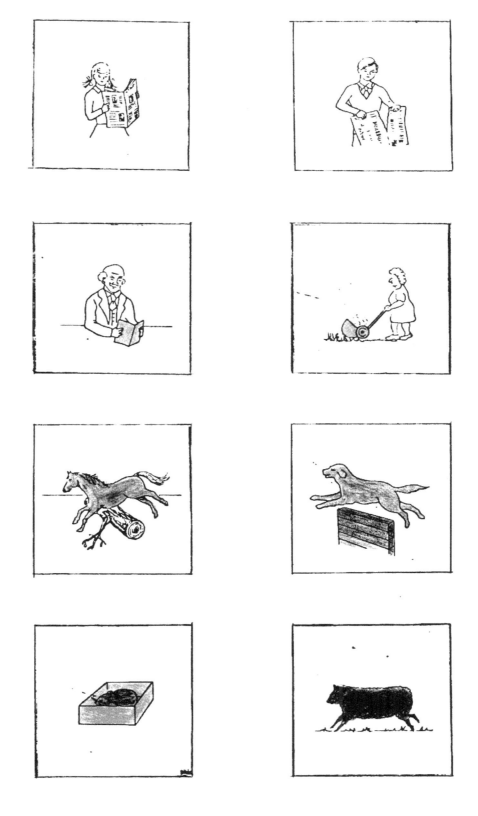

PICTURES 2

Developed after completion
of MSC

The following examples demonstrate exchanges which might be obtained using PICTURES1DICTIONARY, PICTURES1-SYNTAX and the PICTURES1 domain.

1.   THE OLD MAN IS SITTING ON A BLUE CHAIR

      good
      Good
      GOOD

2.   THE BROWN HORSE IS NICE

      good
      Good
      GOOD

3.   THE WOODEN CHIAR IS BLUE
                  ?????
      I do not know the word "CHIAR"
      Do you mean "CHAIR" ? Y/N   ?

4.   THE BROWN HOUSE IS NICE
                  ?????
      I do not know the word "HOUSE"
      Do you mean "HORSE" ? Y/N ?   N
      I know only these words which begin with "H" :-
               HUNGRY   HOOP   HORSE

5.   THE OLD MAN SITTING IS ON A CHAIR
              ??? ??????? ??
      good
      BUT either a word is missing
              or the words are in the wrong order

6.   THE CHAIR IS OLD AND RED

      good
      Good
      BUT   The chair is not red

7.   THE BIG BLUE HORSE IS NOT BEHIND A TREE

      good
      Good
      BUT   The horse is not blue
      and   The horse is behind a tree

Chapter V.   Discussion.

V a) Program design.

A number of minor problems have been mentioned in the appropriate
sections of chapter IV.   Many of the problems relate to robuust-
ness.   Perhaps the most important are i) the danger of entering words out of hash position when using the 'query and/or amend'
option of MAKEDICTIONARY; ii) the danger of an infinite loop if
any attempt is made to exceed the dictionary's capacity; iii) the
inability of MAKESYNTAXFILE to alter existing syntax files and
iv) the duplication of feedback during 'suggestword' and following semantic analysis.   These problems are the result of hurried
design due to the short time available for the project.   They
should be easy to rectify and could be included in a full system
revision which should now be carried out.   The revision should
also involve consideration of the following, more important points.

There are, at present, four programs.   Two would probably suffice.
One program should be a preparation program for use by the teacher,
and would combine MAKESYNTAXFILE , MAKEDICTIONARY and MAKESEMAN-
TICS.   The second program should be the interactive program
based upon MAINPROG for use by the pupil.

The separate existence of the dictionary and the spelling file
is unsatisfactory.   It should be possible to save disk space
by designing a single file which could be accessed both directly and indexed-sequentially,   This might be achieved by re-org-
anising the dictionary into alphabetic sections which could each
be read sequentially, thus dispensing with the spelling file,
and any record of which could be accessed directly by a revised
hashing algorithm.   This should not result in unacceptably
longer 'suggestword' response times.
The semantic array of each dictionary record is limited to a

fixed size. In most records this space is unused while in others it is insufficient. This problem might be overcome by using variable length records, but this solution could result in input/output errors caused by insufficient disk space to insert a newly enlarged record. Input/output errors could be avoided by completely rewriting sections of the dictionary after adding semantic information, and this might be a useful technique for a dictionary sectioned as described in the last paragraph. An alternative solution to the problem of a fixed size semantic array would involve overflow handling techniques for the storage of excess semantic information. However, any solution must preserve the high speed at which information is at present read in from the dictionary.

The representation of syntax types in integers is clumsy, making it necessary for the teacher to keep a list of syntax types and their integers while preparing syntax files and dictionaries. This could be avoided by replacing the integers with an enumer- ated type. An enumerated type consists of a list of identifiers which could be used to represent syntax types more meaningfully.

Similarly, the negative integers which represent semantic rules might also be replaced by an enumerated type. However, semantic rules are possibly unnecessary. In PICTURES 1 SYNTAX they could be avoided by introducing three different syntax types for present participle, in place of the one which currently exists.

The separation of syntactic and semantic analysis imposes limits to the complexity of language which can be processed. If these limits are above the requirements of the envisaged application then all is well, but if the system is unable to operate at the required level a new approach may be needed.

The present approach has the advantage of simplicity. It is easy for a teacher to design new syntactic exercises by simply constructing a new network diagram. The introduction of additional procedures to perform semantic checks is also straightforward. Furthermore, a finite state grammar presents no error recovery problem during syntactic parsing.

There are a number of possible ways to increase the complex-language handling capacity of the system. These would all, almost certainly, require the introduction of a more complex method of syntactic analysis. This might involve the use of split-nodes containing more than one separate path, i.e. a node would be associated with more than one successors list, the operative successors list being determined by the path into the node. This technique would dispense with the awkward syntax type transformations performed by MAINPROG. Paths between nodes might be associated with semantic checking procedures thus performing syntactic and semantic analysis in one pass. But the benefits of any improvement would need to be weighed against the loss of any advantage arising from the present simplicity of the system.

The appearance of the system would be improved by the use of screen graphics instead of external pictures. The written interaction could then take place below the picture. Domains such as PICTURES 1 would not be suited to this because they consist of more than one picture, but single picture domains, perhaps even using animation, could be designed.

V b) Linguistic processing.

By no means can LUCALD be regarded as a natural language processor. Finite state grammars seem adequate for handling simple and retstricted syntax, but more complex language would demand such extensive program support that the approach would become

70

impracticable. However, LUCALD does not need to be able to process every imaginable syntactic convolution in order to be a useful classroom aid. Its viability depends upon its capacity to deal with those aspects of language which would help a deaf person to function in society.

So far the program has been tried with only one syntax file which includes certain variations on the present/active/transitive sentence form. Other simple syntax files can almost certainly be constructed with equal results. But even within these limitations, some problems of linguistic processing have not been overcome. In order to convince many educators of LUCALD's classroom potential, the following kinds of problem may have to be dealt with successfully :-

i) Irregular grammatical behaviour. For example, in the following sentences the noun 'grass' behaves plural and singular respectively.

" The sheep is eating grass",

"The grass is green".

"Sheep" can present similar difficulties.

ii) Semantic differentiation between more than one object of the same kind. If a picture contains two horses then it seems essential to be able to determine to which horse a sentence refers.

iii) The use of the definite versus the indefinite article. Correct usage is a matter of incredible delicacy depending on such factors as the number of objects and previous reference.

It may not be necessary to be able to deal with all difficulties of this kind. Some may be avoided by careful selection of pictures and exercises. But of central importance is the number of problems which cannot be overcome. If this is high then it may be necessary to adopt a different method of linguistic processing, or to even abandon the "language understanding" computer assisted learning approach altogether .

<u>V c)</u> Feedback.

i) Form :   It would seem, in the absence of experimental evidence , that the form of feedback for lexical and semantic errors is adequate.   But because deaf children experience particular difficulty with syntax, syntactic feedback must be improved. It is not sufficient to simply underline every out of sequence word pair, and then to give a single error message to the effect that either a word has been omitted or that the words are wrongly ordered.   The underlining should be retained but some attempt to give differential error messages should be made.

At present three syntactic error marks are used in the sentence array.   Using these fully it is possible to give alternative messages for sentences which have not been properly started or completed.   Some attention should be given to the possibility of extending the error mark system so as to give different messages for errors occurring within the sentence. This should not be difficult for errors which are isolated, common or confined to one phrase.

An additional way to give syntactic feedback is by the generative use of the semantic representation.   By taking the main semantic components of an erroneous sentence (i.e. subject and object nouns; verb) it should be simple to construct an approximation to the leaner's intention.   This could then be presented in a similar way to that of spelling corrections.   Even when one of the semantic components is absent it might still be possible to make suggested sentences.   This would require the use of database techniques to organise the semantic information so that,

for example, an unknown verb which links two given nouns could
be found.

ii) Accuracy: Inaccurate feedback may be divided into two
categories; either the learner is not told when he has made a
mistake, or he is told that he has made amistake when in fact
he has not.   Provided that the dictionary and syntax file have
been properly prepared it is unlikely that an uncorrected mistake
could pass through the system.   The real problem is the second
kind of inaccurate feedback.

The learner, being more intelligent than the computer, will
occasionally behave in a more complex linguistic way.   He might,
for example, respond to picture 4 of the PICTURES 1 domain
(Fig 15) with the sentence-
> "Each of the four circular wheels is divided
> radially by spokes into six equal segments"

or the learner might make a semantic abstraction
> " My little brother has a blue pram".

To tell the learner that this is wrong could actually reverse
previous progress.

In LUCALD this is not entirely avoidable. Certain safeguards
should be taken: the careful matching of dictionary and syntax
file to the leaner's level of ability; appropriate tutorial
guidance so that the leaner's aims are compatible with the
dictionary and syntax file; and the availability of a supervis-
ory human teacher for consultation when the learner is in difficulty. These measures may avoid the problem but they do not
resolve it.   The danger of confusing the pupil with inaccurate
feedback is still present and this would have to be considered
against any benefits to be gained by using LUCALD.

V d) Tutorial considerations

The work carried out so far provides a central program which could be used for different purposes by different tutorial systems.   Language games and specific syntactic exercises have been mentioned as possible applications.   For some applications a scoring mechanism would be a useful addition to the system.

It is unlikely that the learner will be prompted to enter any sentence at all.   Chapter $\overline{V}$c.mentions the importance of guidance. But too much guidance , the elicitation of a completely predict- able sentence by, for example, demanding a reply to a specific question, would not make full use of LUCALD's capabilities. A prompting method which required the learner to construct a sentence choosing words from a list of suggested vocabulary would be one compromise between the two extremes.   This would be particularly useful if a count was kept of the words used by the learner so that words unused so far could be suggested. It might also be possible to extend this idea to certain syntac- tic structures.

A scoring mechanism might also be used to give general performance feedback to the learner, thus stimulating interest and motivation.

A second tutorial consideration concerns the three-level approach to analysis and therefore to feedback.   It seems pedantic to insist on the retyping of a whole sentence following a single, simple spelling mistake.   It might be better to ask correction of the erroneous word only, and to then proceed with syntactic and semantic analysis using an automatically amended sentence. Similarly, after a simmple syntactic error, the JUMBLE approach of allowing sentence rearrangement by single key entry of initial letters might be usefully incorporated.

$\overline{V}$ e.   Potential and usefulness.

It is difficult at this stage to assess the potential usefulness
of LUCALD as a classroom aid.   There is no explicit experimental evidence supporting the whole psycholinguistic rationale on
which the system is based, and development is not yet sufficiently
advanced for trials with deaf children.   Provided that most of
the difficulties can be overcome, LUCALD wouldseem to have at
least a similar potential to that of ILIAD.

The main strength of LUCALD is in its ability to work with the
self-constructed sentences of deaf children.   It then only
attempts to guide correction of errors actually made by the
children.   It does not, unlike JUMBLE and some ILIAD exercises,
present erroneous sentences for the children to correct.

An important feature is the program's capacity to work with
different dictionaries and syntax files thus enabling a wide
range of vocabulary, syntax and pictures (semantic domains) to
be used.   By this approach many of the problems in developing
a comprehensive language processing system have been avoided.

The main disadvantage of utilising restricted but interchangeable
dictionaries and syntax files is that the leaner's responses
must occur along carefully guided lines.   This tends to make
LUCALD an "analytical" rather than a "natural" teaching tool.
There is a danger of teaching rigid, overstructuredsyntax.   However the possibility that LUCALD could be used to control
linguistic games, and its possession of semantic as well as
syntactic elements, makes some concession to the "natural" method.

A more final assessment of LUCALD can only be made after further
development.   This should be along two lines.   Firstly, the
capacity to handle more complex syntactic structures and semantic

concepts should be developed.   An assessment may then be made

about whether the system can work with those structures

which would provide developmental exercises for deaf children.

Secondly, work should now begin on the tutorial aspects of the

system.   The tutorial aspects give a concrete purpose to the

system, and it is on the achievement of this that most judgment

will be made.

REFERENCES

Aho, A.V. and Ulman, J.D. (1977)
Principles of Compiler Design. Addison Wesley.

Arnold, P. (1978)
The Deaf Child's Written English – Can we measure its
quality ? J.Brit.Assn.Teachers of the Deaf. 2, 196-200.

Arnold, P. (1981)
Recent Research on the Deaf Child's Written English.
Accepted for publication in J.Brit.Assn.Teachers of the
Deaf.

Arnold, P. and Crossley, E. (1981)
Unpublished sample of 78 spelling errors of deaf
children occurring in spontaneous writing about the
pictures of the Sentence Comprehension Test. (Wheldall
et al, 1979).

Arnold, P. and Wildig, S. (1981)
Language Games for Deaf School Children.
Accepted for publication in Teaching English to the Deaf.

Bates, M. and Wilson, K. (1979)
A generative computer system to teach language to the
deaf. In Proc. 1979 ADCIS Conference, Association for
the Development of Computer-Based Instructional Systems.

Bates, M. and Wilson, K. (1980)
Language Instruction Without Pre-Stored Examples.
Paper presented to the Third Canadian Symposium on
Instructional Technology, Vancouver, February 1980.

Bates, M., Beinashowitz, J., Ingria, R. and Wilson, K.
(1981) Generative Tutorial Systems.
Paper presented at the ADCIS Conference, Atlanta,
Georgia. March 1981.

Bonvillian, J.D., Charrow, U.R. and Nelson, K.E. (1973)
Psycholinguistic and Educational Implications of Deafness.
Human Development 16, 321-345.

Brennan, M. (1976)
Can Deaf Children Acquire Language ? An evaluation of
linguistic principles in deaf education.
Supplement to The British Deaf News, February 1976.

Bunch, G.O. (1979)
Degree and manner of acquisition of written English
language rules by the deaf.
American Annals of the Deaf, 124, 10-15.

Bunch, G.O. and Clarke, B.R. (1978)
The deaf child's learning of English morphology.
Audiology and Hearing Education, 4, 12-24.

Bundy, A., Burstall, R.M., Weir, S., and Young, R.M.
(1978) Artificial Intelligence : An introductory course.
Edinburgh University Press.

77

Clark, R.A. and Sewell, D.F. (1979)
Why can't the deaf read ? Some comments on Gormley and
Franzen. American Annals of the Deaf, 124, 847-8.

Conrad, R. (1977).
The Reading Ability of Deaf School Leavers.
Brit.J.Ed.Psychology, 47, 138-148.

Crystal, D. (1979).
Working With LARSP. Edward Arnold, London.

Dale, D.M.C. (1974)
Language Development in Deaf and Partially Hearing
Children. Thomas, Springfield Ill.

Francksen, K. (1980).
Language Difficulties of the Congenitally Deaf.
The Behavioural Sink, no. 10. Dept.Psychol., Univ. Hull.

Gormley, K.A. and Franzen, A.M. (1978)
Why can't the deaf read ? Comments on asking the wrong
question. American Annals of the Deaf, 123, 542-547.

Hoemann, H. (1976)
The spelling proficiency of deaf children.
American Annals of the Deaf, 121, 489-493.

Levinson, S.E. and Liberman, M.Y. (1981)
Speech Recognition by Computer.
Scientific American, 244, 56-68.

McNeill, D. (1970)
The acquisition of language : the study of developmental
psycholinguistics. Harper and Row, London/New York.

Moores, D.F. (1978)
Educating the Deaf. Ch. 11.
Houghton Mifflin, Boston.

Myklebust, H.R. (1965)
Development and Disorders of written Language, Vol 1,
The Picture Story Language Test.
Grune and Stratton.

Pollack, B.W. (1972)
Compiler Techniques. Auerbach.

Quigley, S.P., Power, D.J. and Steinkamp, M.W. (1977)
The Language Structure of Deaf Children.
Volta Review, 79, 73-84.

Raphael, B. (1976)
The Thinking Computer - mind inside matter.
Freeman, San Francisco.

Sandals, L.A. (1976)
Computer Assisted Learning with the Handicapped.
Paper presented to the Western Industrial Research and
Training Centre Workshop and Conference 'Preparing the
Retarded for Life in Society'.

Sewell, D.F., Rostron, A.B., Phillips, R.J. and
Clark, R.A. (1979)
Mini-computers as aids for assisting in the linguistic
development of deaf children. Teacher of the Deaf,
J.Brit.Assn.Teachers of the Deaf, 3, 36-41.

Sewell, D.F., Clark, R.A., Phillips, R.J. and
Rostron, A.B. (1980)
Language and the Deaf : An interactive microcomputer
based approach.
Brit.J.Educational Technology, 11, 57-68.

VandenBerg, D.M. (1971)
The Written Language of the Deaf Child.
New Zealand Council for Educational Research.

Wheldall, K., Mittler, P. and Hobsbaum, A. (1979)
Sentence Comprehension Test.
NFER Publishing, Windsor, Berks.

Williams, F.A. (1959)
Handling Identifiers as Internal Symbols in Language
Processors. Communications of the A.C.M. 2, June 1959.

Winograd, T. (1972)
Understanding Natural Language. Academic Press, New York.
also in Cognitive Psychology, 3, no.1.

Wirth, N. (1976)
Algorithms + Data Structures = Programs, Prentice Hall.

www.ingramcontent.com/pod-product-compliance
Lightning Source LLC
Chambersburg PA
CBHW081227050326
40689CB00016B/3702